NARCISSISTIC PERSONALITY DISORDER IN RELATIONSHIPS

How to Make a Narcissist a Better Man

FIDELMA RAFFERTY

© **Copyright 2016 by Fidelma Rafferty- All rights reserved.**

The follow book is reproduced below with the goal of providing information that is as accurate and reliable as possible. Regardless, purchasing this book can be seen as consent to the fact that both the publisher and the author of this book are in no way experts on the topics discussed within and that any recommendations or suggestions that are made herein are for entertainment purposes only. Professionals should be consulted as needed prior to undertaking any of the action endorsed herein.

This declaration is deemed fair and valid by both the American Bar Association and the Committee of Publishers Association and is legally binding throughout the United States.

Furthermore, the transmission, duplication or reproduction of any of the following work including specific information will be considered an illegal act irrespective of if it is done electronically or in print. This extends to creating a secondary or tertiary copy of the work or a recorded copy and is only allowed with express written consent from the Publisher. All additional right reserved.

The information in the following pages is broadly considered to be a truthful and accurate account of facts and as such any inattention, use or misuse of the information in question by the reader will render any resulting actions solely under their purview. There are no scenarios in which the publisher or the original author of this work can be in any fashion deemed liable for any hardship or damages that may befall them after undertaking information described herein.

Additionally, the information in the following pages is intended only for informational purposes and should thus be thought of as universal. As befitting its nature, it is presented without assurance regarding its prolonged validity or interim quality. Trademarks that are mentioned are done without written consent and can in no way be considered an endorsement from the trademark holder.

Table of Contents

INTRODUCTION 1
CHAPTER 1 What is Narcissistic Personality Disorder? 3
CHAPTER 2 Symptoms and Warning Signs 5
CHAPTER 3 Narcissism in Romantic Relationships 11
CHAPTER 4 Women, How to Deal with Your Narcissistic Man . 17
CHAPTER 5 How to Heal from a Narcissistic Relationship 21
CHAPTER 6 Overcoming Narcissism 27
CONCLUSION 31

INTRODUCTION

Congratulations for purchasing *Narcissistic Personality Disorder: How to Make a Narcissist a Better Man*.

It is said we are not to seek love that love finds us. Relationships of all kinds are a beautiful thing! The more time is spent with people, the bigger and better the foundation of all life's relationships with others should become. But occasionally, we all run into at least a couple people who tend to do their best to not make the best better, but rather to selfishly belittle and destroy their relationships piece by piece. And the sad thing is, some of them do not even realize that they are the reason those foundations crumble and why so many people have walked away from them.

Have you ever heard of the term "narcissist"? If not, this book will explain what it is in depth. And if you have heard this term coined and actually believe you are in love or are dealing with a vainglorious individual in your life, you have come across the right book to set you on a path to try to help these people, as well as yourself.

The following chapters will discuss what narcissistic personality disorder is, the warnings to watch for when self-diagnosing, steps to help those with these symptoms come out of their closet of self-involvement, what to do in both non-romantic and amorous relationships, when it is time to seek professional assistance, the process in mending rocky relationships, and last but not least, learning to love yourself again after the games you had no choice but to play from these toxic people.

There are plenty of books on Narcissistic Personality Disorder on the market, thanks again for choosing this one! Every effort was made to ensure it is full of as much useful information as possible, and hope this book leads you to happier relationships in all parts of your life!

CHAPTER 1

What is Narcissistic Personality Disorder?

We are all human. And in the world today, as humans we are made to think that everything has to be perfect. In tip-top shape, and there is no rooms for error. Well, we weren't created like mechanical robots. We were, however, built with faults. Some have many, some have only a few. But our imperfections are what make us individuals! We can rest assured that there is no one person out there that is an exact copy of who we are, inside or out.

In saying that, it is of human nature to be a bit selfish and conceited from time to time. But in this book, we are to discuss people who are overtaken by these two emotions, among other symptoms that are rather negative.

A **narcissist** is an individual who have a very excessive admiration of themselves, and are only interested in what can be done to suit their fancy.

This lack of empathy for others and exaggerated vanity of self is definitely not a new development is the human race. This term was actually coined and created from a mythological Greek youth, by the name of Narcissus, who was beyond infatuated by his own reflection in a lake. Unfortunately, personal mirrors were not invented during this time. Narcissus was said to have fallen in love with his reflection, not knowing it was him. He died, for the grief of finding out that the one he had fallen so deeply for did not actually exist outside of himself.

It started with a man, and is not surprisingly seen in more men than women.

Narcissistic Personality Disorder or NPD is a persisting pattern of bizarre behavior defined by exaggerated feeling of self-importance, the hardcore desire for admiration and a lack of understanding for other people. Individuals who have these symptoms are also controlled by an excessive need to achieve power, look perfect and manipulate others to get ahead in their endeavors. The signs usually are seen in early adulthood, but are seen among an array of scenarios.

The reasons and causes of NPD are still unknown. This disorder affects males more than females, and is seen heavily in younger individuals rather than older people. About 1% of people are said to be affected by NPD at some point in their lives, and doesn't necessarily begin during the early years of being an adult. Diagnosis by a healthcare professional can tend to be a recommended choice. However, therapy after being diagnosed can be rather difficult, for those who are narcissistic do not see anything wrong with themselves as people.

Within the following chapters you will find the symptoms to look for, the proper measures to self-diagnose, as well as learn tips to deal with the narcissistic men that may be or have invaded your life.

CHAPTER 2

Symptoms and Warning Signs

It is important to live by the rule of "sticking with your gut feelings." If you think your man is extremely self-involved, and plays you as a pawn in his self-absorbed games, it is time to really seek out and find the tall-tale signs of what his issue may really be. That said, there is a major difference between being narcissistic and actually exhibit the mental disorder NPD. If you can note just a few of the following symptoms, he may just be narcissistic. If he exhibits most of the symptoms below, then it might be highly likely he has narcissistic personality disorder.

Narcissistic Symptoms

- Are the people involved in his life often upset with him?
- Is it hard for him to maintain and keep relationships?
- Does he put himself before others always?
- Talks about himself a lot?
- Craves attention and admiration from others?
- Exaggerates his achievements?

- Sets unrealistic goals?
- Believes he is beyond special?
- Fast changing mood swings?
- Does not tend to take the feelings of others seriously?
- Does whatever he can to win?
- Dreams of unlimited power, money and/or success?

Although narcissists tend to have a high self-esteem on the outside, the story on the inside does not match up. He probably has a very deep lack of security. He wants to live a life that makes others envious, but tends to realistically be the jealous one in the picture. Any relationships that are not family ties tend to be short-lived and rocky. Even though he is easily hurt, he has no problems hurting the feelings of others. And when hurt, tends to act out in rage. It is often a very narrow one-way street with these individuals. He can take and take, but does not have any intentions of giving back.

There are many people who hold some of these narcissistic traits, but do not let them disrupt their lives enough to hold a disorderly title.

Associated Feature of NPD

Along with the tendency to eagerly exaggerate their skills and accomplishments, people who have narcissistic personality disorder consider themselves to be the highest on the social totem pole. They tend to be very impatient when people talk about themselves, and interrupt conversations often. This leads those with NPD to unknowingly hurt others with their devaluing words to other people within the conversation as well. When they do realize that they maimed someone else's feelings, they act in contempt, viewing others as weak. But when their ego is hurt by any type of criticism, they tend to act disproportionate to the circumstances at hand. Even during times of insecurity, their self-image still remains intact.

While others exhibit the above types of symptoms, there are also people who show more pathological narcissistic traits. This can mean they are controlling, do not tolerate the views of others, unaware of the needs of those around them, point blame constantly and are persistent in trying to convince people in seeing them how they want to be seen.

Causes of Narcissistic Personality Disorder

There is no actual one cause for the birth of NPD in people. It is usually a concoction of environmental, social, genetic and neurological factors that play together in their separate roles to create this unpredictable show.

Genetics – There is some evidence that points to heredity in being a cause for some NPD symptoms. It is seen quite often in male twins, one being more susceptible to having the traits that may lead to NPD than their birth brother. But an actual pinpointed gene has yet to be determined to watch for in humans that will lead those to more than likely be narcissistic.

Environmental Factors – It is much noted that the biggest and most prominent factors that influence the onset of narcissistic behaviors are social and environmental factors. Flawed attachments from a child's primary caregivers can result in a child's misperception of themselves, causing them to think they are in no way connected to those that surround them. As they grow older, they have a tendency to believe that they are unwanted by others. And the opposite is true was well. Parents who hover over their children, who are insensitive or over-controlling can warp a child's brain to create false perceptions of themselves in various ways. The following traits have been studied by many researchers as factors that highly promote the development of NPD.

- Contentious temperament at birth
- Extreme admirations that has never been balanced with feedback from others
- Unreasonable praise for good behavior or extreme criticism for bad behavior
- Overindulgence by parents, other family members and/or peers
- Being praised for looks by adults
- Emotional abuse during the course of childhood
- Unreliable care giving
- Learning manipulative ways from peers or parents
- Regulates self-esteem through the level of value from parents

It seems in today's world of self-righteousness around every corner, there has been a major increase of children who exhibit the traits that make them at high risk for developing narcissistic personality disorder. All kinds of cultural elements can come into the picture and be stirred around, attached and branched off any of the above traits.

Parents of children, this paragraph is for you! People wonder how people become narcissistic. Well, usually tends to start at a very young age. It is important to lead your kids to go do great things that you will be proud of, but their achievements should not be just about you! Often, narcissistic people were neglected children, who's parents were more focused on themselves that they could not wholeheartedly attune to the needs of their child. The child was only deemed as useful when they could help their parents with something they were trying to achieve. In saying all this, take a break from working at home when you have already been at work all day. Play with your kids, learn THEIR interests, make them hobbies you can work on and achieve together. Otherwise, you kids are going to be left with an emotional hunger that will trail on into their adult lives, and reek havoc on the lives of other innocent people.

Neurobiology – Recent research has finally started to see a pattern in those with NPD symptoms, as well as structural abnormalities in the brains of these individuals. It seems that within the brains of these people, there is less gray matter in certain areas of the brain, which affects the balance of emotions. The regions of the brain that are the most effected by this lack of grey matter deal with regulations of emotions, compassion and empathy for others, as well as some cognitive functioning.

Types of NPD

Unprincipled – Lacking of a conscience, disloyal, dominatingly deceptive, "con artist", vindictive

Amorous – Sexually seductive, hinder real intimacy, craves decadent desires, pathological lying

Compensatory – Lack of self-esteem, creates illusions to appear superior, often appreciates results from self-enhancement, seeks to counteract feeling inferior

Elitist – Feels as though they are somehow privileged in status, seeks a favored life, cultivates special statuses by association

Malignant – Guiltless, feels no remorse, aggressive, expects betrayal and seeks out punishment, has a craving for revenge, isolated, often suicidal

Attention – Believe attention should always be on them, go out of their way to capture the attention of others often

Beyond the Rules – Believes they are absent from having to follow the rules

CHAPTER 3

Narcissism in Romantic Relationships

The facts of narcissistic behaviors do not stop with just family and friends, the most vulnerable of places narcissism is seen is within loving, romantic relationships. Usually just seen in one partner, there are times it is seen in both, making for a very unhealthy relationship as a whole. We are living in an ever increasing narcissistic world, with the "pay attention to me" mentality that is fueled by outside factors such as social media. With this increase, there are more and more people who dive head first into relationships with these individuals without knowing it at first. As a narcissist's true colors start to shine, that is when their significant other begins to realize they have fallen for one. The thing in romantic relationships is, you more than likely love that person, and do not want to leave them. Within this chapter we shall discuss how narcissism appears in the romantic setting, as well as how to deal with your narcissistic partner.

A romantic relationship with conceited individuals is often compared to being on a haunting roller coaster ride with Jekyll and Hyde, with intense highs and lows. The main reason we connect with people on a deeper level is to bond with others. But narcissists do not gain romantic relationships for this reason. They are usually unable to 100% feel love, and lack the capability to truly connect and form normal attachments with others. But when their entire sense of self is dependent of the admiration of others, they are in need of people. They view people as more of a commodity than actual human beings.

Narcissists are forever living with deep voids inside them. The only things that fill such voids are the temporary love and esteem that is stemmed from another. Those that are characterized as narcissists often say that they are never satisfied for long periods of time, always on a mission to find the temporary fix to fill whatever craving they have at the time.

Oblivious to the wants and needs of other people, they enter relationships in the attempt to fill their temporary desires. They often look for those that are always available for sex, can stroke their ego or whatever else they crave. Relationships with narcissistic individuals are often described in three phases, listed below.

The Over-evaluation Phase

When choosing their next "victim", people affected by narcissism pick those carefully, usually by status. Anyone who is attractive, popular, gifted in some way that suits their fancy, or rich are highly targeted. The bigger the status, the higher the value, at least as seen by a narcissist.

Once someone is chosen, narcissistic people get into a tunnel vision type of living, in the pursuit of whom they picked, they will represent themselves in the most perfect image possible. In this phase, they tend to be excessively caring and loving, giving their targets truckloads of attention and compliments that sweep their victims right off their feet, into their arms for the taking.

Narcissists in this stage are very euphoric, as if on cloud 9. They idolize their targets by speaking of them often, and have big hopes and dreams. They believe they have found their soul-mate. This is sadly the closest that narcissistic people get to feelings love. This would be classified as infatuation by many others who do not exhibit permanent narcissistic behaviors.

The Devaluation Phase

This phase is when a narcissists mark is wiped off and when their significant others start to really see their true colors and what they are made of. The shift of behaviors has said to been either gradual or practically overnight for some. The attention they once gave you is gone, substituted with silence. Days and weeks could go by and you do not hear from them. This leaves a narcissist's victim wondering where the heck they went wrong.

The thing about narcissists is, they become bored easily. This is because that never-ending void we talked about earlier, needs to be filled yet again by something new. They are addicted to that euphoric high from the over-evaluation phase. They believed you were special, but not they don't think you are, because why would their void still be there if you were?

The blaming game starts, as they become ever so moody and agitated at the slightest of things. In attempts to create distance between them and you, they give you the silent treatment, which often makes the targets cling a bit to the narcissist in an attempt to understand and mend the relationship. But the harder one clings, the harder they pull away, and as they do this, they treat the target like a punching bag, criticizing and blaming them for everything.

The targets become an emotional wreck, for their narcissist significant other has left the relationship for no apparent reason. They use your misery as food to feed off of. It is the same as getting fueled by your admiration; it is not seen much differently by them. Targets try their damnest to try to seek out the person they so profoundly fell in love with before the mask was removed, to no avail. The thing is, that kind, caring individual you once cared for never really existed. It was an act to secure you to supply them with the tools they needed to temporarily fill their void(s). Heartbreaking, isn't it?

Narcissists continually treat victims like pedals of a flower, chanting "I love you" and "I love you not" for as long as the victim of their careless acts allows them to do so. They will come in and out of your life indifferently, as if nothing happened, just to see you suffer as they lure you back in time and time again.

Either the narcissist finds another target to sink their teeth into, or you will get sick of fighting for someone that is psychotic and no longer fighting for you and leave.

The Discard Phase

It is quite the sight to watch the phases of a narcissist, and how they can change overnight, pulling away as you grasp harder. Once their supply from you has dried up, they are on to the next, leaving major havoc in their wake. It is quite the task, getting over the relationship that one had with a narcissist. Victims are left with a shattered self-image, and picking up the pieces from all the hurt that this person who doesn't have a real conscience left. Recovering from narcissistic relationships will be discussed in ....

It is important to be vigilant, and not fall back in the grasp of the narcissistic person you used to love, for there are chances they may return to feed off of you some more. Once free, triple lock the door to yourself, which includes cutting all ties. Otherwise, you can end up like the many people in situations where they go through these three phases over and over and over again. And trust me, it is not fun.

I loved a narcissistic individual for three and a half years of my life, and oh man, can I tell you that those three short years seemed like a decade at the very least. She was charming, affectionate, down to earth...there was nothing to not like about her! For a year out of the three we managed to make a 6 hour long distance relationship work, spectacularly well. For a narcissist, it was a great cover, not having to be around me so she could do whatever she pleased. The mask came off rather quickly when she moved to my city in with me. It was a euphoric couple months, it was great to have closed the gap on our distance. But, she started spending more and more late nights at her pathetic fast food job. She became more distant quickly, keeping her feelings in a lockbox that I no longer had the key to. I then began to catch on to her rapid lies and manipulations, which angered her each time I questioned her. The physical abuse that stemmed from her drug abusive rage to the emotional turmoil that she made me live through, it took awhile, but I finally decided to cut ties. Despite the love I had for her, I could no longer put up with the daily bullshit that overshadowed my life and our relationship due to her careless actions. I cut my losses with her over a year ago, and she still occasionally pokes around to see if she can dig a hole back into my life. It is important to not let their charm sway you, no matter their words and kind actions. It is usually a ploy.

After a lot of personal mending and self-reflection, I can say I loved a narcissistic monster. Everyday was a challenge, but I learned where lines should be drawn, how to build boundaries, and how to once again love the most important person in the world, myself.

CHAPTER 4

Women, How to Deal with Your Narcissistic Man

After reading all of the above information as a woman who suspects their husbands to be narcissistic, you are probably pondering the question of, is he really and truly capable of love?

The sad thing is, he is in a relationship with himself, first and foremost. He views you, his wife, as an extension of himself that you have a duty to fill. Despite all the emotional trials and tribulations he makes you endure, he still always comes back at some point with more charm, excitement and the attention he gave you to initially sweep you off your feet. This leaves you a sense of hope that things are bound to only go up, right?

Life behind closed doors and out in public are like dwelling in two different dimensions with a narcissistic partner. In public, they fully display their charismatic selves, drawing people to them like flies. Yet behind the walls of your home, he criticizes and belittles you, making it a pretty prominent fact that they only love themselves. Which, in reality, ain't quite the case. He actually has very low self-esteem, using flattery and arrogance to cover up with they truly feel inside. They cannot admit their own faults to themselves, let alone others, causing them to be hostile towards themselves, which then leads them back to being hostile towards you, which is no fault but their own.

Narcissistic men also find the need to always be in control, over every single detail of your life. They get envious of others easily, making them wary and questionable when you spend time with others. Some are so bad that they do not even allow you to leave your own home without you receiving consent from them first. This can even lead to an emotional and physically abusive relationship.

So, women, how to go about dealing with your conceited husband? Well, first it is important to recognize what and who you have chosen, and reflect on the motives that he as your husband led you into choosing him as a partner. Many individuals who fall in love with narcissists actually have issues with co-dependency and do not have the confidence to set boundaries and be on their own.

Understanding your role within a narcissistic relationship is vital in the process of being able to truly confront and reflect upon yourself, and then to challenge yourself to change your half of the relationship dynamic. Doing this, in turn, will hopefully make your narcissistic partner to look at themselves and delve a bit deeper into their personal issues.

On the contrary, there are so that are so in depth and comfortable with living within their narcissistic masks that it is almost an impossible task to be able to pull them out of their cemented ways. If you truly love this person and have faith that they can change, there are some things you can do to keep the peace, or begin the process of separating yourself from them.

- Do not contradict or deviate with them

- Learn what matters most to them, and compliment them on those aspects often

- Ensure that most if not all statements are somewhat or all about them, do not mention yourself often

- Do not ask or require intimacy from them (this could also be a good motive to protect you as well)

- Encourage them to talk about themselves. Do your best to act fascinated with the words spewing from their mouth

- Start the process of isolating your finances from theirs, in secret of course.

- Begin to look for emotional support from others, especially from those that may be in the same situation as you

    - It is ideal to maybe create a new profile on social media, a name that they would not recognize or know of. This will help you communicate with current friends, as well as maintain constant assistance from outside sources, such as those in support groups

- Begin to have the state of mind that you are already single, and if you are a parent, a single parent. Take care of your children and the chores on your own, never asking your partner for assistance.

- Last but certainly not least, take quality time to practice self care. It is more than crucial to know and keep your sense of self during this sensitive time.

If you are not planning to cut ties at some point, you are going to have to change some things about yourself that no woman should have to do in a marriage. There is no time like right now to take back what has been stolen by your narcissistic hubby.

If you are to remain married to this sort of man, you are going to have to gain and build a confidence that is strong enough to deflect even the biggest arrows he is going to shoot your way. Having such a confidence will ensure that you remain calm in the toughest of situations, even when he is trying his damnest to break you down to the ground.

You have to keep in mind that no matter what, no matter the scenario, time or place, YOU are the most important person in your life. Your needs do matter, even though your husband doesn't deem them as such or maybe doesn't see them at all. You have been used to being his servant, only taking the crumbs he leaves behind as yours, if there is any. Even though there will be friction, MAJOR friction, you have a right to take the icing from the cake occasionally. You and your needs are just as important as his.

Learn to walk away from the tantrums that narcissistic men tend to throw, sometimes on a daily basis. They want to burst your bubble, to get you on their petty level. No matter the bad looks or grimaces he shows upon his face, or how much rage is in his eyes, just walk away from the situation. Otherwise, you are just fueling his fire, which ignites from upsetting you. If you do not act phased, the little fire he tried to start automatically burns out.

For there to really be any hope of actually recovering from a narcissistic relationship, the person who is the narcissist has to overcome their self-centered and arrogant traits that plague them. They have to have the power to challenge their self-feeding habits and pseudo-independent stances. Developing their capacity to have compassion and empathy for others is vital.

CHAPTER 5

How to Heal from a Narcissistic Relationship

Those who have been in relationships or have been married to people who exhibit narcissistic behaviors know it is a type of emotional hell, and is in fact a form of emotional abuse. This chapter is mainly for those that have managed to find their way out, or for those that are even more frightened by what they should emotionally expect of themselves once they get themselves a safe distance from the narcissist they were once in love with, or may even still be in love with.

"Why is the process of healing so long?", "Why can't I get the person who treated me poorly out of my mind?", "Why do I still love them?", "Will this pain and heartache ever go away?" These may all be questions you are having, and that is perfectly normal.

First of all, congratulations. I know this seems highly inappropriate right now but bear with me. You need to give yourself credit for enduring the life with a narcissist for however long you did for. It is no easy task. Imagine the new found freedom you have now come across. You will be allowed to make your own decisions and become the person you once were or really want to be. And the big secret, who you already are inside of you, has been all along! It is time for you to indulge in the things you love, the things that make you feel great to be alive, without permission, and within guilt. This is the beginning of finding yourself after the abuse from a narcissistic relationship again.

I know what you are pondering now, "what if I am no good at what I think I love or want to do?" Well, what's the hurt in trying? You may be better at it than you think! The thing is, you are used to be torn down. You are used to being controlled, and not able to choose for yourself.

Some people lose their jobs, homes, kids and even their lives obsessing over the emotional turmoil they endured during their time loving a narcissist. Whether you have already walked away or thinking about doing so, it is important to keep in mind that the walking away is deemed to be the easiest part. The personal healing you are about to endure is not going to feel good, especially at first. It will feel a lot like putting salt upon a deep wound. But, it will be worth it, I promise. This chapter is here to discuss coping mechanisms to get you on your well deserved path to mending and shaking hands with the person you have had hidden in the closet of expectations with your now ex-relationship with a narcissist. Good luck.

I will first tell you, you are going to be in disbelief. You may even suffer from Post Traumatic Stress (PTS) because of the abuse you endured. The feelings ARE bound to be more than overwhelming, it will feel like you are drowning, but only at first. Chaotic, terrible, anger, anxious, vengeful...these are just a few things you are about to feel, or may already be feeling. Definitely normal, even though you will feel far from such. These emotions are a part of being human, you are initially grieving the loss of someone you loved. And it is worse, because they are still living.

First, here are some basic steps to assist you in where to start in the process of picking up all the shattered pieces that was left from your relationship.

Accept – it is important to come to terms and accept the situations, and more important, yourself. You will want to blame yourself for things getting out of hand. But you need to recognize you were in a relationship with an individual who had a personality disorder, which in turn is not your fault whatsoever.

Take responsibility – Taking the time to truly realize that you chose this person, and why you did, is important to be able to not land yourself in this type of situation again in the future. Take note that narcissists are liars and manipulators, and often come off as very irresistible. Balancing this out with acceptance is a delicate step.

Cut off contact – This is crucial. This is because at some point, they WILL try to come back and lure you back into their web of lies. This means ALL ways of communication. Leaving a window open for a narcissistic ex to return is detrimental to the healing process, especially if you are gullible to their ways of endearment.

Direct kindness inwards – Often times, we go out of our way to help others. Well, it is time to TAKE time to help yourself, and be kind to all that you are.

There will come a point to STOP the madness – You are not to blame for being treated in the ways you were by this person. Change the words flowing throughout your mind, and they will begin the process of kick starting a positive chain reaction inside of you as well.

Get in touch with your passions – remember and take into account the activities and things you once loved and helped in making you feel absolutely fulfilled. Despite the way it sounds, it is a vital step in regaining your sense of self. Plus, you will feel much happier doing these things, this helping you gain some of that confidence of yours back as well!

Learn more about narcissistic behavior – this will help you pinpoint red flags when coming across and meeting new people, as well as those that are already in your life. It is important to remember that narcissists choose those that are strong, confident, compassionate etc. They are not going to target those that are able to take care and handle their child-like needs and demands. They do not seek people who will not be able to look after them.

Grieving is okay – it is alright to grieve the narcissistic person you once loved. As well as grieving for the person you once were within that relationship. But guess what? You are on the way to creating a better version of yourself rather soon!

It is also okay to be angry, and have nasty feelings. Many have this idea that just because their partner was fake, that their feelings for them were too. No, you are allowed to feel the way you do. You do not need permission for that. Not allowing yourself to process feelings can actually be quite detrimental, and can lead to very negative outcomes later in life, and can lead to long times of bereavement.

One step forward – (and two steps back, some days) each and everyday you need to take a step forward, no matter how baby-sized the step may be. Each of them count into digging yourself out of this hole that you were once in. Listen to yourself, and your heart, and remember that no matter what and no matter how long it takes, you will find yourself once again. There are many times I look back upon my time in a narcissistic relationship, and I have a hard time believing I was in one for that number of years. But, now that I am on the positive end of it all, I am eternally grateful for finally choosing myself to love first and foremost.

It is also okay to seek out professional assistance if you believe you may be suffering from any type of psychological issues. Complicated grief, which is a long-lasting form that takes over every aspect of one's life, is one example of these problems. These types of issues are rather common in these situations, because victims never get the closure they need to truly and 100% move forward with their lives.

With the end of an abusive relationship comes a truckload of unfinished business, whether is be disputes, discreditation of your behavior, unanswered questions or unreturned love, you are left hanging. This leads to those being constantly stuck in pain, and unable to truly complete the closing process of their time with the narcissist.

The motivation of a narcissist is to take away each and every shred of your self-esteem because that is how they keep you attached to their lure, to keep you pondering. They leave you to think, "I am damaged, better to keep them around, because having someone that treats me poorly is better than not having anyone at all." Everything negative they have ever told you, was a lie. You are a beautiful individual who deserves to be loved by someone that deserved you wholeheartedly. From this chapter alone, you are on your way to retrieving your true self from the trenches of despair. Pick yourself up and conquer the world yet again! I dare you.

CHAPTER 6

Overcoming Narcissism

By the process of both recognizing and separating themselves from their inner voices of self-soothing, self-aggrandizing and self-attacking, narcissists can indeed overcome this terrible state of mind that also classifies as a mental disorder. This is no easy task, but it has been seen and done successfully. The attitudes they internalized and have utilized from early childhood are deeply intertwined inside them. But one of the best methods of conquering narcissism is the process of voice therapy.

Voice therapy is a very powerful technique that is able to tap onto a person's negative core beliefs. It identifies negative thought patterns that are in control of the individual's narcissistic behavior. The process of switching the verbalizations into a second person point of view allow the narcissist to separate their own points of view from the hostile point of view back onto themselves. It allows them to receive a taste of their own medicine, in other words. We won't get too far into detail within this book, but just web searching "voice therapy" can provide you plenty of legitimate information about the technique.

Narcissists also need to learn to differentiate the traits that their parents or caretakers still act upon to this day. Being around that behavior only drives them to think they can continue it without too much consequence. This also goes for the adaptations they had to make when their parents neglected them growing up. To be able to break the patterns of their self-centered behaviors, they must do these vital things to be able to get to a path to begin to tread upon. Fighting the urge to compare themselves to the likes of others, as well as the need to be the best and the most perfect all the time is one of the aspects of being a narcissist that is the hardest to overcome.

The process of fostering self-compassion rather than self-esteem is another practice that many have seen success in when it comes to curing narcissists and their behaviors. Self-esteem centers itself on the evaluation of oneself in relation to others, while self-compassion focuses on treating yourself with kindness, recognizing the shared qualities of you versus the rest of humanity, as well as being mindful when pondering over negative aspects of yourself. Studies have actually found that focusing on raining self-esteem actually worsens narcissistic actions and behaviors, as raising awareness of self-compassion combats it. This is because it includes the idea of a shared humanity with other people, leading to thinking about others before oneself.

The process of developing transcendent goals, taking the time to truly invest and care about other people is another hard to do but crucial way to cure narcissism. Having opportunities to be generous to others should be highly sought out for those that want to change their narcissistic ways of life. Living within these corrective opportunities that come to light intensely assist the build of a real, intact self-esteem and practice focusing on others rather than sustaining all of one's energy within themselves only.

Four tips to remember when you start your trek to overcoming your narcissistic ways:

1. Empathy – attempt to put yourself within the shoes of other people. Taking a look at the real world and realizing other people have it tougher than you can get you to take less focus off yourself and your issues and help out others if they need it.

2. Open to Criticism – learn to be polite when you do not like the opinions of other people about yourself or things you do. Do not be close-minded to what others have to think all the time.

3. Learn to Laugh at Yourself – do not beat yourself up if you do not end up living to your own expectations. You are not perfect, and everyone makes mistakes. Laugh at yourself and know you can do better next time.

4. Don't Always Have the Mindset of a Competitor – bragging about everything you have achieved and accomplished is not something people want to hear about 24/7. Learn to remain modest in your successes.

If none of the above techniques do the trick, there is always professional treatment. Getting to the point of recognizing your behaviors and wanting to change them is a big step! With the help of patience, courage and a true commitment to you, therapy is a great option. Therapists can provide boundaries that narcissists would otherwise refuse from their spouses of significant others. With the increase of self-acceptance, processes of psychotherapy have been shown and proven to greatly increase the positive aspects of a narcissist's way of life and quality of living.

CONCLUSION

Thank for making it through to the end of *Narcissistic Personality Disorder – How to Make Your Narcissist a Better Man*. I hope it provided you the information you need to begin the process of whipping your narcissistic husband/spouse into shape!

Living with or around narcissistic individuals is no easy task, and shakes the core of understanding who we are. These people will beat you to the ground in more ways than one, and know exactly how create you into the worst versions of yourself. That is their goal in life, and yours should be to keep your sanity and sense of self worth in tact as you go through the trials and tribulations of a narcissistic marriage, learn the warning signs of your newest significant other, or trying to cope with these kinds of people who have always been in your life and just don't seem to quite leave.

The next step is to put the advices stated within these pages into play. It is time to make a change, whether it is trying to change these impossible to deal with individuals, or knowing when it is best to walk away from the scenario at hand, either way you are going to make the best out of a terrible situation.

Good luck with mending your relationship(s), marriage, and yourself. You are doing yourself a favor!

Thank you again and good luck!

Printed in Poland
by Amazon Fulfillment
Poland Sp. z o.o., Wrocław